KT-524-859

CONTENTS

WATER FOR LIFE

Water is essential for life. It makes up three-quarters of the human body. We can survive days, even months, without food, but we cannot survive more than a few days without water.

Water world

More than two-thirds of the Earth's surface is covered by water. Vast amounts of water fill the seas and oceans. But this water is salty. We need fresh, unsalty water to drink. Water that falls as rain or snow and collects in rivers and lakes is called fresh water. All living things – humans, other animals and plants – need water to stay alive and grow.

Sprinklers water a field of alfalfa sprouts. Without water, no crops can grow.

The view of our planet from space shows that most of its surface is covered by water.

Eco Thought
Over the last 300 years the number of people on Earth has increased by seven times. But the amount of water we use has increased by 35 times.

Farming and industry

In some countries, two-thirds of the water supply is used by farmers. They need it to water their crops and provide drinking water for their livestock. In factories, water is put to all sorts of uses, such as cooling very hot metals or producing electricity.

In the dry land of Chad, Africa, collecting water from wells is a daily task.

Drinking water on tap

People in developed countries take water for granted. They have a continuous supply of drinking water, every day of the year. They use water in their homes for cooking and washing, and in machines such as dishwashers and washing machines. Water is piped into swimming pools and hosed on to dirty cars or dry gardens.

Scarce resource

In other parts of the world, people do not have running water in their homes. They have to struggle to get enough water for drinking and cooking. Some people have to walk many kilometres to reach the nearest tap or well. They must carry all the water they will need for the day back to their homes.

There is only a limited amount of fresh drinking water. As the world's human population increases, so does the demand for water. In the future, everybody will have to use water more wisely.

WATER CYCLE

The Earth's water is 97 per cent salt water and 3 per cent fresh water. Of the fresh water, 17 per cent is free-flowing and 83 per cent is frozen. So only a tiny part of the Earth's water is for people, plants and animals to share. Since the amount of water is constant, we must use the fresh water over and over again.

Taking Part

Place a potted plant on a large saucer of water. Enclose the shoots of the plant in a clear plastic bag. The water is taken up by the roots and carried through the stems to the leaves. See how long it takes for droplets to form inside the bag. The droplets form because water evaporates from the surface of the leaves and condenses on the cool surface of the bag.

Different states

Water is the only substance to exist naturally in three states of matter. Water is found as a solid when it freezes to form ice. It freezes at 0 °C. Above 0 °C, ice melts to form liquid water. When liquid water is heated, it evaporates and turns into a gas called water vapour. Water can evaporate at almost any temperature above freezing. For example, the water in wet washing will evaporate even on a cool day.

Over 80 per cent of the world's fresh water is locked in the polar ice caps.

How clouds form

Water evaporates from the surface of rivers, lakes, seas and oceans, and from the leaves of plants. As water vapour rises, it cools. It condenses back to form tiny droplets of water. Millions of these droplets form rain-clouds. With more moisture, the droplets get bigger then fall to the ground.

An endless cycle

Water droplets that fall from clouds are called precipitation. Some precipitation is soaked up by the ground and plants. Some drains into rivers, lakes, seas and oceans, where it evaporates and the whole process begins again. This is called the water cycle.

Clouds of mist rise above a rainforest in Rwanda. They are formed from water that has evaporated from the trees.

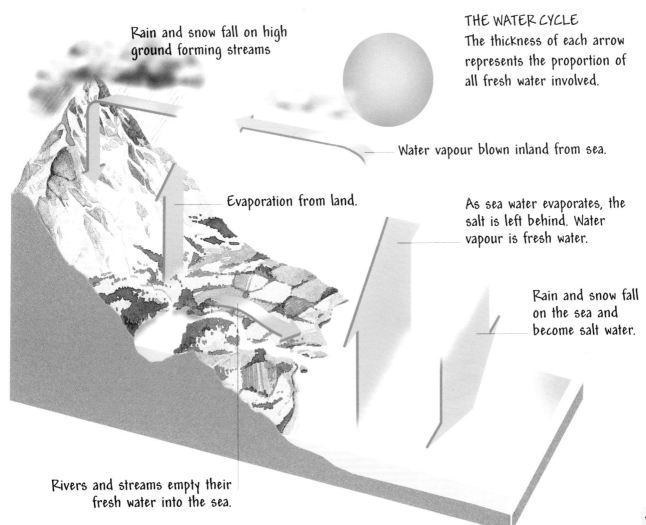

Rain and snow fall on high ground forming streams

THE WATER CYCLE
The thickness of each arrow represents the proportion of all fresh water involved.

Water vapour blown inland from sea.

Evaporation from land.

As sea water evaporates, the salt is left behind. Water vapour is fresh water.

Rain and snow fall on the sea and become salt water.

Rivers and streams empty their fresh water into the sea.

USING SALT WATER

If you lick your lips after swimming in the sea, they taste salty. Salt water is found in the oceans, while fresh water is found in rivers and lakes.

Taking Part

Make 'seawater' by adding 35 grams of table salt to a litre of water. Stir in the salt until it dissolves. Pour some of this salty water on to a saucer. Leave the saucer on a sunny window ledge. The Sun's heat evaporates the water, leaving the salt behind on the saucer.

Salt in water

A litre of seawater contains about 35 grams of salt. Most of it is common salt or sodium chloride – the sort that seasons your dinner – but there are other salts, too. Fresh water contains hardly any salt.

In Sri Lanka, workers build low walls to trap seawater when the tide comes in. The water dries in the Sun, leaving salt for people to harvest.

Life at sea

Too much salt can be harmful. If you drank salt water you would become very ill. But marine animals and plants are adapted to their salty home. Few animals that live in rivers can live in the sea, because they would be killed by the salt water. Salmon and eels are unusual fish because they spend part of their lives in rivers and the rest of their lives at sea.

The green turtle has special glands next to its eyes that remove excess salt from the body.

Making fresh water

In places where water is scarce, rainwater can be collected, stored and used later, and drinking water can be made by purifying seawater. The salt-removing process is called desalination. The water is boiled, causing the water to form water vapour. The salts are left behind and the water vapour is then trapped and cooled so it condenses back into water. The process of boiling and condensing is repeated several times. Each time, the water becomes purer, until finally it is pure enough to use.

Eco Thought

Desalination is an expensive process. It is common in the Middle East, where rich, oil-producing countries can afford to produce vast amounts of water for farming and for gardening. But the poorer developing nations of Africa and Asia cannot afford desalination, even though they have a shortage of clean water. People there must continue to search for fresh water under ground or store rainwater.

In Gibraltar, rainwater is collected to provide water for the local people and the visiting tourists.

RIVERS AND RESERVOIRS

Much of the water we use comes from lakes and rivers. Water companies pump out this water, treat it and pipe it to where it is needed. Where there are no natural lakes, people can make artificial ones.

In this village in Cambodia, a newly-built water system provides much-needed fresh water.

Building reserves

An artificial lake can be made by building a dam across a river. A dam is a barrier that controls the amount of water flowing down the river. In rainy weather, the dam holds back the water and prevents the river from flooding. Water collects behind the dam and forms an artificial lake called a reservoir. Reservoir water can be piped to towns and cities or used to water farmland. This provides people with a year-round source of water.

On the Ground

Each year about 700 new dams are built in the world. The largest-ever dam is being built on the Yangtze River, China. The Three Gorges Dam will be two kilometres long and 100 metres high. It will create a reservoir 600 kilometres long. As well as stopping the Yangtze from flooding, it will also be the world's most powerful hydroelectric dam.

Power from water

Dams can be used to generate electricity. This sort of power is called hydroelectricity. At a hydroelectric dam, water is directed on to spinning wheels called turbines. The turbines drive a generator, which converts the spinning motion into electricity. Hydroelectric power does not produce any pollution. It is also a renewable source of energy, because the water will never run out.

Some problems with reservoirs

Rivers like the Nile in Egypt used to flood each year, fertilizing the fields with silt. Then the Aswan Dam was built. It stopped the floods and the farmers lost an important source of nutrients. They use artificial fertilizers but the land in the valley is not as good as it used to be.

The Owyhee Dam in Oregon, United States, provides electricity to factories and towns.

On the Ground

Dams affect the environment around a river. Rivers carry tiny particles of mud called silt. When a river floods, it dumps the silt on the land. Silt is rich in nutrients and makes the soil fertile. When a dam is built, silt builds up on the bed of the reservoir instead.

In Andhra Pradesh, southeastern India, water is diverted from the River Krishna to provide hydroelectric power. Pylons and cables carry the electricity to towns.

UNDERWATER STORE

When rain falls, it seeps into the soil or runs off into streams and rivers. Water that seeps into the ground is called ground water. It drains deep into the ground until it reaches a layer that it cannot pass through. There, the water collects. Water-filled ground is called an aquifer. The top of an aquifer is known as a water table.

A store of water

Beneath an aquifer is an impervious, or unpassable, layer of rock that stops the ground water draining any deeper. In wet weather, more water collects so the level of the water table rises – the water lies closer to the surface. In dry weather, the level of the water table falls.

This oasis provides water for a holiday resort in Huacachina, Peru.

Springs, oases, wells

When the water table reaches the surface, as at the foot of a slope, water bubbles out of the rocks as a spring. Spring water may collect to form an oasis. The rocks in the ground act as a filter and remove any impurities. Where the water table is under the surface, the water can be reached by digging a well.

Eco Thought

In Mexico City, a water table used to lie close to the surface. So much water has been pumped from the ground, that the rocks immediately beneath the city are now dry. Wells must be dug more than three kilometres deep through impervious rock to reach a new water table.

Women queue to collect water from an artesian well in Malawi, Africa.

Deep water

An aquifer is an underground layer of rock that holds water. The water cannot escape because of impervious layers above and below. In a deep aquifer, the heavy ground pushes down on the water and pressure builds up. When a well is dug down to the aquifer, the pressure is released and the water gushes out of the ground. This is called an artesian well.

Eco Thought

There are many aquifers beneath the Sahara Desert. Water moves along them very slowly. For example, water taken from Egyptian aquifers today may have fallen on the highlands of Ethiopia thousands of years ago when the climate there was tropical and wet.

This diagram shows how the water table can form a spring.

This diagram shows how the aquifer can form a well and an artesian well.

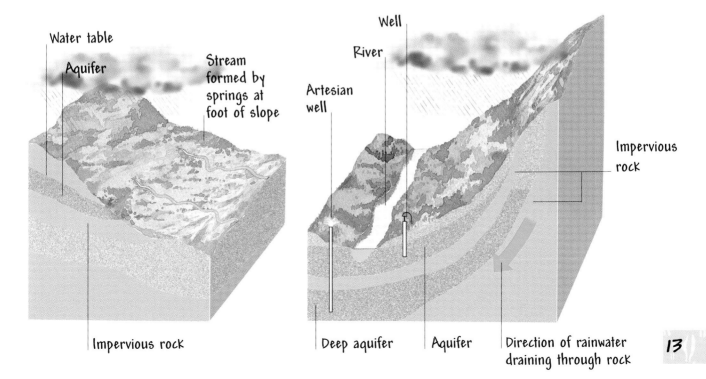

Water table
Aquifer
Stream formed by springs at foot of slope
Impervious rock

Well
River
Artesian well
Impervious rock
Deep aquifer
Aquifer
Direction of rainwater draining through rock

CLEAN WATER

People need clean drinking water. Water taken from deep wells and artesian wells is very clean. It has passed through the ground, which acts as a natural filter.

Dirty water

Water taken from rivers and reservoirs is not clean enough to drink. It may contain tiny, microscopic organisms called bacteria. Most bacteria are harmless, but some cause serious diseases, such as cholera and dysentery. The water may also contain grains of sand, or organic matter from decaying leaves and animal bodies. It may be polluted by sewage or industrial waste. Before it is safe to drink, the water has to be treated.

Reservoir water goes to a treatment plant before it is piped into our homes.

Taking Part

Take a large plastic bottle and cut off the top third. Make a few holes in the bottom. Fill the bottle with clean sand to within ten centimetres of the top. Pour soapy water on the sand. Compare the soapiness of the water that you pour in and that drips out of the bottom of the bottle. The sand filters the impurities out of the water.

Water for drinking

At a treatment plant, water is piped into settling tanks. Here, any large particles in the water sink to the bottom. Then the water passes through a filter. The water is crystal-clear by now, but it may contain bacteria. Bacteria are killed by bubbling chlorine gas though the water, which can give tap water a chlorine taste – like swimming-pool water. The clean water is stored ready to pipe into our homes.

In the United Kingdom, 25 per cent of clean, treated water is lost because of leaky water pipes like this one.

Safe to drink

Unfortunately, in many parts of the world, especially in developing countries, people do not have a supply of safe drinking water. Their wells may not be deep enough and there are few water treatment plants. They may use water from polluted rivers and lakes. The water has to be boiled to make sure all the bacteria are killed. Aid agencies are helping these people by digging deep wells, from which they can collect clean water.

An African girl drinks fresh water from a pipe.

WASTE WATER

The dirty water from baths, toilets and kitchens is called sewage. Once, this was emptied straight into rivers and seas. In some places this still happens. Fortunately, more treatment plants are being built to deal with the increasing amounts of sewage.

Sewage treatment

Sewage and dirty water from homes and factories are piped to waste water treatment plants. First, the sewage is passed through a screen, rather like a giant sieve. This removes large objects, such as pieces of paper and plastic. Then the sewage enters a large settling tank, where the solids sink to the bottom. Finally, the liquid is sprayed over a bed of stones. Here, bacteria and other tiny organisms added to the bed feed on any organic matter in the water. Once the liquid has passed through this bed, it is safe to be pumped into a river.

Farmers' friend

The solid sludge left in the settling tank is moved to a closed tank where it is broken down by other bacteria. This process is called sludge digestion. Digested sludge makes an excellent fertilizer for farmers' crops.

Workers at a waste treatment plant test the water to see how clean it is.

On the Ground

Plants such as reeds can be used to purify water. Reeds grow in shallow fresh water. Sewage can be piped into special reed beds, where bacteria in the water break down the sewage. This produces nutrients which are used by the reeds. The water that drains away from the reed bed is safe to empty into streams and rivers.

At this treatment plant in Brazil, water is being sprayed on to a bed of stones. Here bacteria will digest any remaining organic matter.

Carp ponds

In some countries, sewage is pumped into shallow ponds where bacteria feed on the sewage. After a few days, water is pumped from the first pond into a second, then into a third, and so on. The water in each pond gets cleaner because more sewage has been broken down by the bacteria. Water in the final pond is safe to empty into rivers or the sea. People sometimes keep large goldfish called carp in the ponds. The fish eat the sewage and, in the end, the people eat the fish.

A series of ponds containing water plants provides habitats for different types of bacteria. These are able to break down organic matter in the waste water.

POLLUTED WATER

Not all waste water is treated before entering rivers and seas. Fertilizers and pesticides may drain directly from farmland. Farm slurry (animal waste), sewage and waste water from factories may enter rivers accidently. When people pour paints, bleach and oil down the drain, these too may end up in the local river. All these wastes may carry harmful chemicals.

On the coast of northern Europe, partly treated sewage pours directly into the North Sea.

The manufacture of products that we use every day results in vast amounts of waste, dirty water.

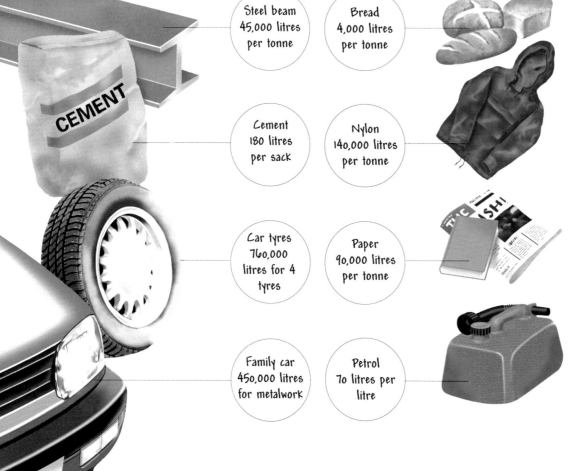

Steel beam
45,000 litres
per tonne

Bread
4,000 litres
per tonne

Cement
180 litres
per sack

Nylon
140,000 litres
per tonne

Car tyres
760,000
litres for 4
tyres

Paper
90,000 litres
per tonne

Family car
450,000 litres
for metalwork

Petrol
70 litres per
litre

On the Ground

One of the world's worst oil spills occurred in Prince William Sound, Alaska in 1989, when the tanker Exxon Valdez struck a reef. Almost 50 million litres of oil spilled out into one of the most unspoilt regions of North America. The oil spread 750 kilometres down the coast, killing 250,000 birds and thousands of marine mammals.

Cleaning up

In many countries, there are laws controlling water quality. Industries have to make sure that waste water emptied into a river does not contain harmful chemicals – otherwise they are fined. Rivers that were polluted are being cleaned up. Fish, such as salmon and trout, are returning to rivers, a real sign that the waters are clean again.

Polluting the seas

Pollution can enter the sea from industries built on the coast or near estuaries, such as paper mills and oil refineries, and from accidents such as oil spills. Also, the world's oceans have been used as dumping grounds for all kinds of waste, often because it is cheaper than having to dispose of waste on land. This damages all marine life, from tiny bacteria to the largest whales. To stop this from happening, there are now international laws that prevent people from dumping waste at sea.

Scientists in the Arctic take water samples to test for pollution.

WATER AND FARMING

Plants need water to grow. When there is not enough rain, farmers water their crops so they grow well. Watering crops is called irrigation. Irrigation is common in the drier parts of the world.

This Indonesian boy waters rows of tender young crops by hand.

Water channels and sprinklers

Irrigation water must be fresh not salty. If plants are watered with sea water, they die from salt-poisoning. The traditional way to irrigate crops is to dig a series of trenches across the fields and fill them with water raised from a well or local river or that has been collected in a reservoir. The water seeps from the channels into the soil.

Nowadays, enormous mechanical sprinklers are a common sight in fields. Irrigation water is pumped from deep in the ground and sprayed over the crops from circular or long, thin sprinklers. From the air, the irrigated fields look like huge green circles or rectangles.

Eco Thought
The world's farm animals include cattle, sheep, pigs, goats and chickens. Together, they use 60 billion litres of water each day. That is enough to fill 120,000 full-size swimming pools.

Trickle and drip

In hot weather, irrigation water can evaporate. To prevent this, farmers use a network of pipes to water each plant individually. The water drips on the soil around the plant and trickles down to the plant's roots. The shade of the plant's leaves stops the water from evaporating. But this only works for larger plants. It is not practical for watering a whole field of wheat, for example.

Water flows along irrigation channels in this field in California, in the United States.

An irrigation channel snakes through the dry Californian landscape.

0890872

Eco Thought

The Aral Sea in Central Asia was once a vast, inland saltwater sea, but now it is shrinking fast. Dams were built on the main rivers that empty into the Aral, so that the river-water could be used to irrigate the cotton fields. Now so little water is reaching the Aral Sea that it may disappear completely by the year 2020.

Salty soil

Irrigation can cause problems. All soils contain salts, but salt levels can increase when soil is poorly irrigated. As water evaporates from the surface of the soil, the salts are left behind. Over a long time, the soil becomes so salty that it is useless for growing crops. This process is called salinization.

WHEN RAINS FAIL

Some dry parts of the world may get rain only once or twice a year, and even these rains are very unreliable. Some years, the rains fail completely. If this happens, the area may suffer from a drought.

Disastrous drought

Drought causes crops to fail. Without their crops, the local people run out of food. Animals die of hunger and thirst. Soon there is a famine. Unless they receive help, the people can suffer from starvation and die.

Helping the hungry

There are many aid agencies around the world, such as the Red Cross. These supply food to areas in times of famine. During a famine, people often have to leave their homes and move to aid camps where they can get food and water. They are so weakened by hunger that disease spreads quickly, and medical help is needed too. The area will continue to need help until the rains return and the first crops are harvested.

Vital supplies of food and medicine are flown into drought-stricken Sudan, Africa.

Deserts, such as the Kalahari, are the driest places on Earth. These oryxes died of thirst.

Eco Thought

The driest area of the world is the Atacama Desert which lies along the west coast of Chile, South America. It had no rain for 400 years, from 1571 until 1971. Rain is still scarce and years without any rain are common.

In Burkina Faso, people are planting trees to help the soil hold more water.

A better solution?

To help avoid famine, farmers can be taught new ways of growing crops in dry conditions. For example, farmers usually clear the stones from their fields, but now scientists have found that it is better to leave the stones. The stones create cool and shady spots to shelter tiny seedlings. Another solution is to plant trees. Once they are grown, they will help to shade the crops and hold water in the ground with their roots.

On the Ground

The Sahel lies south of the Sahara Desert in Africa. To combat drought, farmers who live on sloping land are cutting huge steps called terraces. Terracing prevents the water running down the slopes after heavy rain and carrying away the valuable soil.

CHANGING CLIMATE

The Earth is getting warmer. This is called global warming. This has been happening slowly for many years, but now the process is speeding up.

The greenhouse effect

Global warming is happening because there are more greenhouse gases, such as carbon dioxide and methane. The gases act like the glass in a greenhouse, trapping heat in the atmosphere so that it cannot escape into space. The gases are produced in many ways – they are given off by car exhausts, or when large areas of forest are burnt.

On the Ground

Bangladesh is a low-lying country. If the sea levels rise, much of it would be flooded, causing 13 million people, or 11 per cent of the population, to move to higher land. More than one-fifth of the country's rice-growing land would be flooded, as would two major ports. Powerful tropical storms would become more common and they would flood even more land.

Steam and the greenhouse gas carbon dioxide stream out of the chimneys of this power station in the United Kingdom.

Storms ahead

One effect of global warming may be to change the world's pattern of rainfall. Many areas will become drier. In other areas, there will be more severe storms such as gales and hurricanes. Stormy weather brings heavy rain and flooding. Flooding can devastate crops, destroy towns and kill people.

After an unusually heavy rain, this river in Cambodia burst its banks, flooding the countryside.

Rising sea

As temperatures rise, ice at the North and South Poles may melt, filling the oceans. Already, as the water in the oceans gets warmer, it is expanding and taking up more space. This is raising sea levels and flooding low-lying land with salt water. In the future, this could leave areas of salty land that are useless for crop-growing.

Forward planning

Global warming may cause water shortages in many parts of the world. The deserts and dry areas of the world could expand. Countries in southern Europe, for example, could become drier and hotter. New reservoirs can be built, but they will take many years to fill, so governments will have to act in good time.

This Kenyan farmer lost his sunflower crop to drought. Global warming could make drought more common.

WATER SHORTAGES

People everywhere are using more water. As living standards improve, people use more water – and this leads to shortages.

Lake Mono, in California, is being slowly emptied as it supplies nearby cities with water.

Swimming pools are a wonderful luxury, but they use up precious reserves of clean, fresh water.

On the Ground

Los Angeles does not have enough water. The California State Water Project transports water from Lake Oroville in north California, where there is plenty of water, to Los Angeles, a distance of 170 kilometres over the mountains.

Holiday resorts

People are taking more holidays. Hot places, such as the Middle East and parts of Africa, have increasing numbers of tourists. Hotels are being built and they use up water. Often, hotel guests have more water available in their bathrooms than the local people have to meet all their everyday needs. Tourist attractions such as aquaparks and theme parks also use up precious water. Local water supplies may run out during the busiest times. The water may be turned off during the day, to reduce the amount that people use.

Saving water

There is no shortage of seawater, so more fresh water could be produced in desalination plants. But these are very expensive to build. They also cost money to run because they use large quantities of energy.

The best and cheapest way forward is to conserve as much water as we possibly can. People in the developed world not only use, but also waste, the most water. They are the ones who must cut down on wastage so that supplies of fresh water do not run out.

Water for wildlife

Sometimes, it is possible to get new supplies of water by digging deeper wells or building new dams and reservoirs. But these methods mean that other places go short of water. Wildlife can suffer as oases and watering holes dry up. Fish die as rivers, ponds and lakes dry up. Frogs and toads have nowhere to lay their eggs, and crocodiles and turtles have nowhere to cool themselves.

AVERAGE DAILY USE OF WATER AROUND THE WORLD

City-dweller in the USA - 300 litres

City-dweller in Nigeria - 140 litres

Village-dweller in India - 30 litres

Village-dweller in Madagascar - 6 litres

In the developed world, people use far more fresh water every day than in places where water is scarce.

WHAT CAN WE DO?

There is only a limited supply of fresh water and it has to be used wisely. Everybody must help to save water, even if they live in a part of the world where there seems to be plenty of it.

Helping at home

Do you run the tap while you are cleaning your teeth or washing your hands? Think about the amount of water that disappears down the plug hole. It is much better to only turn on the tap when you need the water. Every time you flush the toilet you use water. Your water company can help you to find ways of reducing the amount of water used with each flush. In Europe, all new toilets will have to be 'low-flush' by law. Baths use up water too – if you can, take a shower instead.

Collect rainwater in a water butt. You can use it to water your plants.

Taking Part

If you have a shower in your bath you can see how much water you save by using it. When you shower, keep the plug in the bath. When you finish, make a note of the level of the water in the bath. Next time, have a bath and compare the water levels.

Instead of using a hose to clean the family car, use a bucket. That way, you are less likely to waste water.

On the Ground

The hot dry weather of the Mediterranean in summer attracts lots of tourists. Conserving water is very important. Signs in hotel bathrooms tell tourists to turn off dripping taps and save water.

Considering others

On a global scale, countries must consider the impact of building dams or taking water from lakes and rivers that they share with other countries. Developed countries must pass on their skills and technology so that poorer countries can develop efficient and constant water supplies.

In areas of the world such as the Middle East and eastern Europe, where supplies of fresh water are limited, governments are now making international long-term agreements that will ensure that each country has its fair share of water.

In Burkina Faso in Africa, local people are storing water from a well in huge tanks to ensure a constant supply of fresh water.

FACT FILE

Water wants

Water demands are increasing rapidly, with up to 80 per cent required for irrigation, less than 20 per cent for industry and just six per cent for people.

New York story

A person living in New York City, United States, uses about 300 litres of water each day. A Kenyan only uses five litres a day.

Water within

The body of a teenager contains about 35 litres of water.

Fatal thirst

As many as 3,500,000 children world-wide die each year from drinking unclean water.

Melting ice

If all the ice in the world was to melt at once, the sea level would rise by more than 60 metres, flooding low-lying areas.

Fake lake

The largest artificial lake in the world is Lake Volta in Ghana, created by the Akosombo Dam. The shoreline is 7250 kilometres long.

Salty land...

There are about 270 million hectares of irrigated land in the world. That is an area the size of India. Almost one-third of this land is damaged by salinization.

...and salty water

The Great Salt Lake in Utah, United States, and the Dead Sea in Israel both have so much salt in them that it crystallizes on their shores.

Recycling in space

In 1973, the US space station, Skylab, went into space carrying just 3,000 litres of water. This had to last the crew three months so it had to be recycled more than six times.

A costly drink

To produce a litre of bottled mineral water costs 1,000 times the cost of a litre of tap drinking water. European sales of mineral water have doubled in the last ten years. Britons drink an average of 8 litres of mineral water a year, but the Germans and French drink more than 100 litres.

Flush it out

The very first toilets with a water flush system, which existed as long as 4,000 years ago, emptied into pits in the ground. The Romans were the first to empty their sewers into rivers, which caused water pollution.

Population problem

In Cairo, Egypt, over 11 million people have to make do with a water supply and sewage system that were developed for a population of 2 million.

Leabharlann Contae na Midhe

GLOSSARY

Aquifer A layer of rock that acts as a store of water. The ground above and below the aquifer is impervious, so water cannot move up or down.

Atmosphere The layer of air that surrounds the Earth.

Bacteria Tiny single-celled organisms. Some can help to break down organic matter such as sewage.

Condense A change in state from gas to liquid, for example, water vapour changes back to liquid water.

Desalination Removing salt from seawater to create fresh water.

Developed country A country that relies on industry and where factories provide more jobs than farming.

Developing country A country that relies on farming, rather than manufacturing goods for export.

Drought A long period without any rain, leading to shortages of water.

Evaporate To change from liquid to gas. Rain evaporates as it is heated by the Sun.

Famine A situation in which there is not enough food to feed the people. People may starve to death.

Fertilizer Nutrients added to the soil to make crops grow faster or bigger.

Global warming The increase in the temperature of the Earth.

Greenhouse gas A gas that traps heat, causing the Earth's temperature to increase. Carbon dioxide and methane are greenhouse gases.

Ground water Rainwater that has seeped into the ground and become stored in the soil or underground rocks.

Hurricane A powerful tropical storm bringing strong winds and heavy rain. It is also called a cyclone or typhoon.

Impervious Impassable. Describes rock that water cannot pass through.

Irrigation Artificial watering of crops, using surface channels, pipes or sprinklers.

Nutrients Chemicals that plants or animals need for growth and health.

Organic Relating to a living thing. For example, organic waste is waste from a person, an animal or plant.

Pesticide A substance that will kill pests, such as greenflies.

Reservoir An artificial lake that stores a large quantity of water for cities and farming.

Salinization When the soil becomes too salty for plants to grow there.

Sewage Semi-liquid waste carried away from buildings, including the waste from the toilet and dirty water from the washing machine.

Silt Tiny particles of rich mud carried by a river or dumped on a valley during a flood.

Slurry Liquid waste, including urine, from farm animals.

Turbine A wheel that is turned, for example by a stream of water, in order to drive a generator and make electricity.

Water table The level in the ground below which everything is saturated with water, so water cannot drain any deeper.

INDEX